EXERCISE YOUR
Find The Dog
Challenge Games

02 - FIND 5 DOGS IN THE PICTURE

03 - FIND 5 DOGS IN THE PICTURE

04 - FIND 5 DOGS IN THE PICTURE

05 – FIND 4 DOGS IN THE PICTURE

06 - FIND 5 DOGS IN THE PICTURE

07 - FIND 5 DOGS IN THE PICTURE

08 - FIND 5 DOGS IN THE PICTURE

09 - FIND 5 DOGS IN THE PICTURE

10 - FIND 4 DOGS IN THE PICTURE

12 - FIND 5 DOGS IN THE PICTURE

15 - FIND 5 DOGS IN THE PICTURE

17 - FIND 5 DOGS IN THE PICTURE

23 - FIND 5 DOGS IN THE PICTURE

25 - FIND 5 DOGS IN THE PICTURE

27 - FIND 5 DOGS IN THE PICTURE

28 - FIND 5 DOGS IN THE PICTURE

33 - FIND 6 DOGS IN THE PICTURE

34- FIND 5 DOGS IN THE PICTURE

35 - FIND 5 DOGS IN THE PICTURE

37- FIND 5 DOGS IN THE PICTURE

ANSWER

01 - FIND 5 DOGS IN THE PICTURE

02 - FIND 5 DOGS IN THE PICTURE

03 - FIND 5 DOGS IN THE PICTURE

04 - FIND 5 DOGS IN THE PICTURE

05 - FIND 4 DOGS IN THE PICTURE

06 - FIND 5 DOGS IN THE PICTURE

07 - FIND 5 DOGS IN THE PICTURE

08 - FIND 5 DOGS IN THE PICTURE

09 - FIND 5 DOGS IN THE PICTURE

10 - FIND 4 DOGS IN THE PICTURE

11 - FIND 5 DOGS IN THE PICTURE

12 - FIND 5 DOGS IN THE PICTURE

13 - FIND 5 DOGS IN THE PICTURE

14 - FIND 5 DOGS IN THE PICTURE

15 - FIND 5 DOGS IN THE PICTURE

16 - FIND 5 DOGS IN THE PICTURE

17 - FIND 5 DOGS IN THE PICTURE

18 - FIND 5 DOGS IN THE PICTURE

19 - FIND 5 DOGS IN THE PICTURE

20 - FIND 5 DOGS IN THE PICTURE

21 - FIND 5 DOGS IN THE PICTURE

22 - FIND 5 DOGS IN THE PICTURE

23 - FIND 5 DOGS IN THE PICTURE

24 - FIND 5 DOGS IN THE PICTURE

25 - FIND 5 DOGS IN THE PICTURE

26 - FIND 6 DOGS IN THE PICTURE

27 - FIND 5 DOGS IN THE PICTURE

28 - FIND 5 DOGS IN THE PICTURE

29 - FIND 5 DOGS IN THE PICTURE

30 - FIND 5 DOGS IN THE PICTURE

31 - FIND 5 DOGS IN THE PICTURE

32 - FIND 5 DOGS IN THE PICTURE

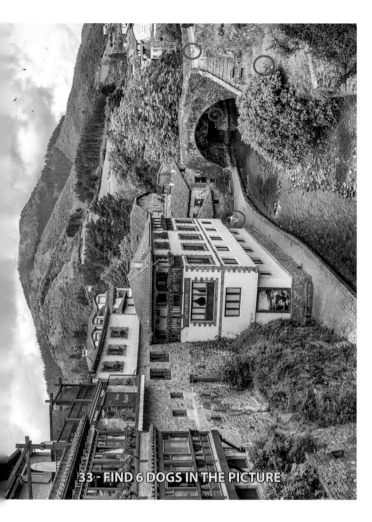

33 - FIND 6 DOGS IN THE PICTURE

34- FIND 5 DOGS IN THE PICTURE

35 - FIND 5 DOGS IN THE PICTURE

36 - FIND 5 DOGS IN THE PICTURE

37- FIND 5 DOGS IN THE PICTURE

38 - FIND 5 DOGS IN THE PICTURE

39 - FIND 5 DOGS IN THE PICTURE

40 - FIND 5 DOGS IN THE PICTURE